ENDANGERED ANIMALS OF
AUSTRALIA,
NEW ZEALAND,
AND PACIFIC ISLANDS

WORLD
BOOK

a Scott Fetzer company
Chicago
worldbook.com

Staff

Executive Committee

President
Donald D. Keller
Vice President and Editor in Chief
Paul A. Kobasa
Vice President, Sales
Sean Lockwood
Vice President, Finance
Anthony Doyle
Director, Marketing
Nicholas A. Fryer
Director, Human Resources
Bev Ecker

Editorial

Associate Director,
Annuals and Topical Reference
Scott Thomas
Managing Editor,
Annuals and Topical Reference
Barbara A. Mayes
Senior Editor,
Annuals and Topical Reference
Christine Sullivan
Manager, Indexing Services
David Pofelski
Administrative Assistant
Ethel Matthews
Manager, Contracts & Compliance
(Rights & Permissions)
Loranne K. Shields

Editorial Administration

Senior Manager, Publishing
Operations
Timothy Falk

Manufacturing/ Production

Director
Carma Fazio
Manufacturing Manager
Sandra Johnson
Production/Technology
Manager
Anne Fritzinger
Proofreader
Nathalie Strassheim

Graphics and Design

Art Director
Tom Evans
Senior Designer
Don Di Sante
Media Researcher
Jeff Heimsath
Manager, Cartographic Services
Wayne K. Pichler
Senior Cartographer
John M. Rejba

Marketing

Marketing Specialists
Alannah Sharry
Annie Suhy
Digital Marketing Specialists
Iris Liu
Nudrat Zoha

Writer

A. J. Smuskiewicz

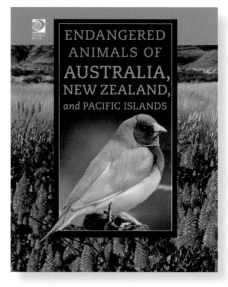

The cover image is the endangered Gouldian finch.

World Book, Inc.
233 North Michigan Avenue
Chicago, Illinois 60601 U.S.A.

For information about other World Book publications, visit our website at **www.worldbook.com** or call **1-800-WORLDBK (967-5325).**
For information about sales to schools and libraries, call 1-800-975-3250 (United States) or 1-800-837-5365 (Canada).

Library of Congress Cataloging-in-Publication Data

Endangered animals of Australia, New Zealand, and Pacific islands.
   pages cm. – (Endangered animals of the world)
   Includes index.
   Summary: "Information about some of the more important and interesting endangered animals of Australia, New Zealand, and the Pacific Islands, including the animal's common name, scientific name, and conservation status; also includes a map showing the range of each animal featured; and a glossary, additional resources, and an index"– Provided by publisher.
   ISBN 978-0-7166-5623-4
   1. Endangered species–Australia–Juvenile literature. 2. Endangered species–New Zealand–Juvenile literature. 3. Endangered species–Islands of the Pacific–Juvenile literature. I. World Book, Inc.
QL84.7.A1E53 2015
591.68099–dc23

2014019655

Endangered Animals of the World
ISBN: 978-0-7166-5620-3 (set)

Printed in China by Shenzhen Donnelley Printing Co., Ltd. Guangdong Province
1st printing October 2014

Contents

Why species in Australia, New Zealand, and Pacific Islands are threatened

The development of Australia's native wildlife is closely linked to the geologic history of that island continent. Hundreds of millions of years ago, all of Earth's continents were connected in one land mass, called Pangaea. About 200 million years ago, the southern part of Pangaea broke away, becoming the modern-day land regions of Africa, Antarctica, Australia, India, and South America. For a time, Australia was still connected to South America, and animals were able to move between these lands. That is why, today, animals known as *marsupials* are found only on those two continents. (A marsupial is a mammal that carries its developing young inside a pouch in which young are *nursed* [fed milk].)

Some 1,500 *species* in Australia, New Zealand, and Pacific Islands are threatened, many critically. (A species is a group of animals or plants that have certain permanent characteristics in common and are able to interbreed.) Of course, this number includes only those species known to science. Many species remain undiscovered. And almost certainly, a number of these animals are in peril or have even disappeared.

Human effect. Australia's animal life began to change after people arrived there, roughly 50,000 years ago. Those first settlers, known as the Aboriginal People of Australia, brought a kind of dog called a dingo with them. Some dingoes escaped into the wild, and today their descendants prey on such native animals as wallabies, woma pythons, numbats, and woylies.

Australia's wildlife changed even more after Europeans began to settle there in the 1700's. The descendants of animals these settlers introduced are often considered major pests and predators today. For example, introduced cats and foxes have killed huge numbers of native birds and other small animals. In addition, many *habitats* have been eliminated by the development of farms and cities. (A habitat is the kind of place in which an organism usually lives.)

New Zealand and New Guinea. The wildlife of New Zealand, an island country about 1,000 miles (1,600 kilometers) southeast of Australia, was similarly affected by human settlers. Polynesian settlers and British immigrants introduced plants and animals and changed the landscape by farming, grazing, and other activities. A similar story played out in New Guinea, an island just north of Australia.

On all three islands, human activities have drastically changed in a relatively short time *ecosystems* that evolved over many years. (An ecosystem is made up of a community of plants and animals and their physical environment.) Native species have often suffered because of these activities.

In this volume. The species presented in this volume represent a variety of endangered animals in Australia, New Zealand, and Pacific Islands. From the smallest and simplest to the largest and most powerful, the continent's wildlife is facing challenges from human beings.

Scientific sequence. These species are presented in a standard scientific sequence that generally goes from simple to complex. This sequence starts with insects or other *invertebrates* (animals without backbones) and then fish, amphibians, reptiles, birds, and mammals.

Range. Red areas on maps indicate an animal's *range* (area in which it occurs naturally) in Australia, New Zealand, or Pacific Islands.

Glossary. Italicized words, except for scientific names, appear with their definitions in the Glossary at the end of the book.

Conservation status. Each species discussed in this book is listed with its common name, scientific name, and conservation status. The conservation status tells how seriously a species is threatened. Unless noted differently, the status is according to the International Union for Conservation of Nature (IUCN), a global organization of conservation groups. The most serious IUCN status is *Extinct*, followed by *Extinct in the Wild, Critically Endangered, Endangered, Vulnerable, Near Threatened,* and *Least Concern*. Criteria used to determine these conservation statuses are listed to the right.

Other designations are based on Australia's Environment Protection and Biodiversity Conservation Act 1999 (EPBC) or the New Zealand Threat Classification System (NZTCS). The organizations use different criteria when assigning their statuses.

Conservation statuses

Extinct All individuals of the species have died

Extinct in the Wild The species is no longer observed in its past range

Critically Endangered The species will become extinct unless immediate conservation action is taken

Endangered The species is at high risk of becoming extinct due to a large decrease in range, population, or both

Vulnerable The species is at some risk of becoming extinct due to a moderate decrease in range, population, or both

Near Threatened The species is likely to become threatened in the future

Least Concern The species is common throughout its range

Icons. The icons indicate various threats that have made animals vulnerable to extinction.

Key to icons

 Disease

 Habitat disturbance

 Habitat loss

 Hunting

 Overfishing

 Pet trade

 Pollution

 Ranching

Ornithoptera alexandrae

Conservation status: Endangered

When seen from the ground, Queen Alexandra's birdwing butterfly might easily be mistaken for a bird. The largest butterfly in the world, it can have a wingspan of up to 11 inches (28 centimeters).

Male birdwings are smaller than females but much more brightly colored. The wings of males have iridescent blue-green streaks over a mostly black background. (Iridescent surfaces change color depending on the angle from which they are viewed.) Females, by contrast, have wings that are brown with yellowish blotches. In both sexes, the abdomen—the long, rear part of the body—is bright yellow.

Queen Alexandra's birdwing butterfly

Development. The *caterpillars* of this *species* (type) are also strikingly colored. They have many bright red spines—and two yellow spines in the middle—sticking up from their black body. (A caterpillar is the second stage in the life history of butterflies and moths.) The caterpillars hatch from yellow-orange eggs that the female lays on leaves of a certain vine that spreads throughout rain forest trees.

The caterpillars feed on this vine as they grow, for approximately 77 days. When a caterpillar reaches its maximum size, it forms a hard, brown shell called a chrysalis over its body. Inside this shell, it undergoes a *metamorphosis*—that is, it changes form and becomes a beautiful butterfly. The butterfly breaks out of the chrysalis after about 42 days.

Discovery. Western scientists first became aware of Queen Alexandra's birdwing in 1907. In that year, Walter Rothschild, a member of the British Parliament and a famous collector of biological specimens, described the butterfly based on a dead specimen. He had received the specimen from a hunter who had shot the butterfly out of the sky in Papua New Guinea (roughly the eastern half of the island of New Guinea). Rothschild named the species after the

United Kingdom's queen at the time, who was Alexandra, the wife of King Edward VII.

Dangers and threats. Queen Alexandra's birdwing can be found only within the coastal rain forest of southeastern Papua New Guinea. Biologists believe that the butterfly's remaining *habitat* (living place) is no larger than about 39 square miles (100 square kilometers). The rain forest has shrunk as people have converted the land into palm oil plantations. Some of the butterflies' habitat was also destroyed by a massive volcanic eruption in the 1950's. The volcano's lava and ash killed many of the large, old trees that the butterflies lived in. The combination of ongoing habitat destruction and the long-term effects of that eruption have prevented the population of Queen Alexandra's birdwing from recovering.

Butterfly collectors are another roadblock to recovery. Collecting, killing, or trading these butterflies is illegal. However, their great size and beauty means that some people pay a lot of money to obtain specimens, however they can.

The beautiful Queen Alexandra's birdwing butterfly is threatened by habitat loss and collectors.

Deinacrida heteracantha

Conservation status: Vulnerable (IUCN)
Relict* (NZTCS)

The giant weta is the heaviest insect in the world. Females, which are larger than males, may reach a weight of 2.5 ounces (71 grams). That makes the giant weta about the weight of a small bird. There are 11 *species* (types) of giant weta, and the wetapunga is the largest. It can grow to a length of almost 4 inches (10 centimeters). The wetapunga got its name from the Maori word for *god of the ugly things*. (The Maori were the first people to live in what is now New Zealand.)

Growth and enemies. During the day, wetapungas generally hide in dead leaves or other plant matter. At night, they move around in trees or on the ground, feeding on fresh leaves. Because of their weight, these insects move slowly. They cannot fly or jump to get away from predators. When disturbed or threatened, they make a loud hissing noise by rubbing their back legs against the sides of their abdomen. If the noise does not frighten a predator away, the wetapunga might become a fat meal for a harrier, kingfisher, or other hungry animal. The wetapunga is easiest to attack when it is *molting* (shedding its hard, outer covering). It must molt to grow.

Breeding. Females leave the trees to lay their eggs in the soil. After laying their eggs, the females die. The eggs hatch in from one to four months, depending on how warm and wet the soil is. A wetapunga takes about 18 months to grow to adulthood. But it typically does not breed until near the end of its roughly two-year lifespan.

Habitat. Fossils dating to 190 million years ago show that insects similar to the wetapunga once lived in what is now Australia—when Australia and modern-day New Zealand were connected geologically. The wetapunga was once common

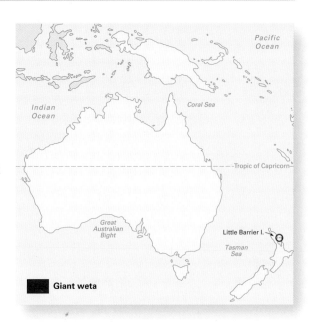

Giant weta

across the North Island of New Zealand and on several offshore islands. Today, the only wild population is found on Little Barrier Island, a small island off the northeastern coast of the North Island.

The insect's population began to plummet as rats, cats, ferrets, stoats, hedgehogs, and other nonnative predators introduced by Europeans spread throughout New Zealand in the 1700's and 1800's. These animals found the slow-moving insects to be easy prey. Furthermore, much of the natural *habitat* (living place) of the wetapunga has been destroyed or *degraded* (reduced in quality) by the clearing of land for agriculture and settlements and by the introduction of such browsing animals as cattle.

Many wetapunga live in *captivity* (zoos or other protected facilities). Fortunately, the species breeds well in captivity, which has increased the wetapunga's odds of survival.

*Occupies less than 10 percent of its former range.

The giant weta, the world's heaviest insect, was commonly preyed on by animals introduced to New Zealand by Europeans.

Gippsland giant earthworm

Megascolides australis

Conservation status: Vulnerable (IUCN)
Vulnerable (EPBC)

You've probably seen earthworms crawling through the dirt or sliding across a sidewalk after a heavy rain. Imagine seeing an earthworm with a body up to 10 feet (3 meters) long and 3/4 inch (2 centimeters) wide, made up of 400 segments. The worm may weigh as much as 14 ounces (400 grams).

The Gippsland giant earthworm is native to an area called South Gippsland, in the state of Victoria in southeastern Australia. It can be found mostly in small, isolated populations and has become increasingly rare. The big worm lives in soils along creek banks and in river valleys, open pastures, and grazing land and cropland. The front part of the earthworm's body is dark purple, with the rest pinkish-gray.

Burrows. These worms spend most of their adult lives traveling rapidly through complex burrow systems, which they make from 3.3 to 5 feet (1 to 1.5 meters) below the surface. They prefer soil that is wet, because the moisture makes it easier for them to slide along and breathe.

As Gippsland giant earthworms travel through the soil, their movements often make a loud gurgling or sucking noise that can be heard above the surface. The worms eat mostly roots and *organic matter* (dead, decayed plant and animal material) in the soil. They sometimes stick their head out of their burrow to feed on plants at the surface.

Reproduction. Like other earthworms, the Gippsland giant earthworm is a *hermaphrodite.* That means that each individual has both male and female reproductive parts. After two worms mate, each worm produces an egg inside a cufflike structure, which surrounds the body. This structure, with the egg inside, then slides off over the worm's head. The buried egg hatches into a young worm after about a year.

Gippsland giant earthworm

Threats. The Gippsland giant earthworm faces many threats. The soils in which they live have been disturbed by the construction of roads and dams, the laying of cables, plowing, and other forms of digging and development. As a result, the soils have dried out and changed in other ways, making burrowing and breathing more difficult for the worms. In addition, some people illegally dig up the giant worms for collectors.

Conservation. Conservationists are working to protect and restore the natural *habitat* of the Gippsland giant earthworm. (A habitat is the type of environment in which an animal lives.) Some worms are protected in *captivity* (a zoo or other nonnatural place in which animals are kept for safety or display and sometimes bred). But, unfortunately, the worms do not breed well under such conditions.

A conservation worker digs up one of a colony of some 800 Gippsland giant earthworms from an area threatened by the construction of a highway. The worms were moved to a safer area nearby.

Glyphis garricki

Conservation status: Critically Endangered (IUCN) Endangered (EPBC)

This medium-sized shark lives in the muddy, fresh water of rivers and in *brackish* (slightly salty) waters near the coast of northern Australia and the southern coast of Papua New Guinea. Males usually reach a length of about 5 feet (1.5 meters), but females may grow to more than 8 feet (2.4 meters) long.

The waters in which the river shark lives are typically dark and unclear, so these sharks do not rely on their eyesight to get around. Instead, the sharks navigate and find their prey by sensing the weak electric fields generated by ocean currents and by muscle movements in other animals. They detect these electric fields with special sensing organs in their head called ampullae (am PUHL ee) of Lorenzini. The sharks have many slender teeth that they use to capture and eat their prey—mainly fish.

Threats. The New Guinea river shark is one of the rarest sharks in the world. Its coastal *habitat* (living place) has been *degraded* (reduced in quality) by damming, mining, and other development projects. Some of these projects, such as mining, have polluted the shark's habitat. Dams have blocked the movement of the shark's fish prey into the waters of its

New Guinea (Northern) river shark

habitat. *Commercial* (business) and recreational overfishing have also reduced the numbers of the shark's prey fish. Some of this fishing involves an illegal activity called gillnetting, in which a large mesh fishing net is set up vertically in the water so that fish swimming into it become entangled and stuck in the mesh by their gills.

Tags attached to the fin of a New Guinea river shark will help scientists collect information about this critically endangered species.

Glyphis glyphis

Conservation status: Endangered (IUCN)
Critically Endangered (EPBC)

The speartooth shark looks similar to the New Guinea river shark. The two *species* (types) differ mainly in the location of their so-called waterline—that is, the part of the body where the darker, upper coloration changes to the lighter, lower coloration. The maximum size of the speartooth shark is not known with certainty. However, scientists have found jawbones that indicate that some individuals may reach a length of 9.8 feet (3 meters).

The speartooth shark has a similar *habitat* (living place) and *range* as those of the New Guinea river shark. (Range is the area in which an animal occurs naturally.) Both sharks face similar threats, though biologists believe that there are probably more speartooth sharks than New Guinea river sharks today.

Conservation. The government of Australia has enacted conservation plans for both the New Guinea river shark and the speartooth shark. These plans include public education programs to increase awareness of the threats

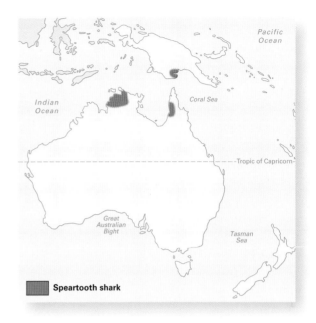

■ **Speartooth shark**

to these species. In addition, biologists are seeking to learn more about the behaviors and ecology of these species to increase their chances of survival.

Efforts to educate fishers about the impact of gill nets on the rare speartooth shark have had considerable success.

Urolophus bucculentus

Conservation status: Vulnerable

"Stingaree" is the name used in Australia for a flat, long-tailed marine fish known as a stingray in North America. The great, or sandyback, stingaree lives off the coast of southeastern Australia. The yellow-brown fish usually stays near the sea bottom, where it hunts mainly for *crustaceans* (hard-shelled animals).

Poisonous spine. The great stingaree may grow to about 35 inches (89 centimeters) long, making it one of the largest stingarees in Australian waters. The disc-shaped body of the animal, not counting the tail, is wider than it is long.

Near the base of the tail is a large spine attached to a poisonous gland. When a fish or other animal—or a person—disturbs the great stingaree, its tail swings upward to jab the disturber with the spine. The spine attack can be as dangerous to a person as a poisonous snakebite. Female stingarees that don't want to be bothered sometimes stab males that are trying to mate with them.

Reproduction. Female great stingarees carry their developing young inside their bodies— somewhat like mammals. But unlike a mammal mother, a stingaree mom does not have a *placenta* to nourish the young. (A placenta is a disk-shaped organ that enables the developing young to obtain food and oxygen from the mother's blood.) Instead, the great stingaree produces a nutritious substance called "uterine milk" for its young. After growing inside the mother for more than a year, one to five young, called pups, are born.

Threats. Huge numbers of great stingarees are caught by *commercial* (business) fishing operations, especially off the coast of the Australian state of New South Wales. As a result, the stingaree population in that area has fallen greatly since the 1970's. The stingarees are

Great (Sandyback) stingaree

usually not the fishers' target, because stingarees do not have much food value. Rather, they often become *bycatch* (animals accidentally swept up by fishers trying to catch more desirable food fish). Sometimes, fishers kill the stingarees they catch out of fear of getting stung. But even stingarees thrown back into the water may be harmed. Simply handling a pregnant great sting-aree can cause its pups to die.

Another problem for conservationists is that stingarees are slow to reproduce. They become sexually mature later in life. In addition, the females carry their developing young for 15 to 19 months, so they produce pups only every other year. As a result, scientists do not expect the stingaree population to rebound quickly, even though the fish are legally protected by Australian laws.

The great stingaree is often a victim of commercial fishing operations seeking more desirable fish species for human consumers.

Litoria booroolongensis

Conservation status: Critically Endangered (IUCN) Endangered (EPBC)

This small, warty, grayish to reddish-brown tree frog grows to a length of about 2.2 inches (55 millimeters). Females, which are a little larger than males, have a smooth white throat. Males have a dark throat. Unlike many other male frogs, male Booroolong frogs do not have a vocal sac, which is a membrane in the floor of the mouth that makes calls louder. The male Booroolong frogs make a soft "qirk qirk qirk" call that resembles the purring of a cat.

Habitat. The Booroolong frog is found mainly along rocky streams in forests and shrublands in southeastern Australia. The frogs also live in some cleared areas that have been turned into pastures or grazing lands. Adults mainly eat insects. *Tadpoles* (immature frogs) eat water plants and algae. Tadpoles grow to a length of about 2 inches (50 millimeters) before undergoing *metamorphosis* (changing from a legless tadpole into a fully adult, legged frog).

Habitat loss. Biologists believe that the Booroolong frog has disappeared from about half of its known native *range* since the 1980's, mainly because of the loss of the water so essential to the frogs' survival. (A range is an area in which a plant or animal naturally lives.) Severe *droughts* (dry spells) in Australia have dried up many streams.

Some of these streams have also been overtaken by weeds and *sediment* (soil or other material flowing from the land into the water), which further *degraded* (reduce the quality of) the frog's *habitat* (living place). The sediment comes mostly from land cleared for agriculture and logging. The dirt and weeds fill up the rock crevices in the streams where the frogs like to lay their eggs. In addition, some of the sediment contains agricultural pesticides and other *toxic* (poisonous) chemicals. The frog has also lost some of its watery habitat

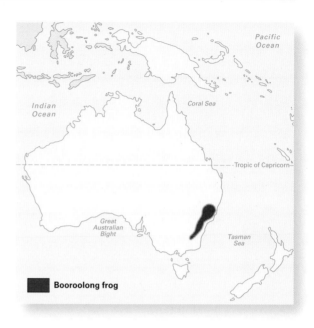

Booroolong frog

because of the diversion of water from streams for farm irrigation and power production by hydroelectric dams.

Fungal disease. Disease has also claimed many Booroolong frogs and other frog *species* (types) in the region. The worst disease, called chytridiomycosis, is caused by an infectious form of fungus called *Batrachochytrium*. Yet another threat to the Booroolong frog comes from European carp, goldfish, and other introduced, or nonnative, fish that kill and eat its tadpoles.

Conservation. Biologists at the Taronga Zoo in Sydney began a captive-breeding program for the Booroolong frog in 2007 using an initial population of 34 frogs. In 2008, hundreds of frogs produced in this program were released into the wild. Australian authorities are also working to restore the natural habitat of Booroolong frogs by removing the sediment and weeds that have destroyed egg-laying sites in streams.

The Booroolong frog has suffered severely from drought and disease.

Aspidites ramsayi

Conservation status: Endangered

The woma python—also known as the Ramsay's python or sand python—is an olive or brownish snake with blackish crossbands. It has small, black, beady eyes on its narrow head, which is about as wide as its neck. This snake differs from most other pythons by not having heat-sensitive pits by its mouth. Such pits help pythons find rodents and other warm-blooded prey in the dark.

Hunting style. Like other python *species* (types), the woma python is a constrictor, meaning that it squeezes its prey to death. Most pythons coil their body around a captured animal and tighten the coils until the prey's breathing and blood circulation stop. The snake then swallows the dead prey whole.

By contrast, the woma python often can't coil its 4.5-foot (1.5-meter) body around its prey, because it captures many of its victims, including small rodents, inside burrows. There is not enough room inside a burrow for the python to wind its full body around the animal. So the snake usually pushes a single loop of its body against the animal, crushing it against the side of the burrow. Then it swallows the animal.

Many woma pythons have scars on their bodies from rodents that fight back. Besides rodents, woma pythons also catch birds, lizards, and other small animals for food. The snakes do most of their hunting at night. During the day, they usually hide in burrows, hollow logs, thick plant growth, or other shelters.

Reproduction. Females wrap their long bodies around their eggs after they lay them. The coils *incubate* the eggs (keep the eggs warm and safe) until they hatch in two or three months.

Habitat. Woma pythons live in dry, grassy plains across much of central Australia. They also live in an area along the country's northwestern coast. Despite this wide *range*,

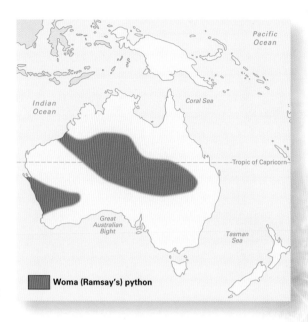

Woma (Ramsay's) python

populations of the python are thinly scattered throughout the region. (A range is the area in which an animal occurs naturally.) Much of the snake's natural grassy *habitat* (living place) has been replaced by wheat farms, other cropland, and grazing land. This habitat destruction has eliminated the python's shelter and prey.

Nonnative foxes introduced into the region by people have also killed many of the pythons and much of their prey. In addition, woma pythons are sometimes captured for sale as exotic pets.

Conservation. An area in the *outback* of South Australia more than 326,000 acres (132,000 hectares) in size has been set aside to protect woma pythons and other endangered species. (The outback refers to the rural interior of Australia and its unique characteristics.) Australian authorities are also educating members of the public about ways to use the land that are less harmful to the snakes.

The woma python has become the frequent prey of foxes introduced to Australia by people.

Ctenophorus yinnietharra

Conservation status: Vulnerable (IUCN & EPBC)

The frightening name of this animal conjures up images of a fire-breathing beast. However, the Yinnietharra rock dragon is really just a shy, reddish-brown lizard. The rock dragon is not very big, growing to a length of only about 3 inches (8 centimeters), including its tail, which is marked by four black bands. Around its neck is a collar of large, pointed scales. This spiked collar helped inspire the "dragon" name of the lizard.

Daily life. Yinnietharra rock dragons spend much of the day basking in the sun on rocks or resting on the limbs of acacia shrubs. The lizards like to munch on acacia leaves. When threatened or even when merely approached, rock dragons are quick to run away and hide. Favorite hiding places include spaces under boulders and inside hollow logs.

The boldest and most aggressive a Yinnietharra rock dragon ever gets is during the mating season. Then, males may lash their tails if females or other males are near. The lashing helps attract females and serves to scare away other males.

Habitat. As far as scientists can tell, the Yinnietharra rock dragon lives in two small areas of rocky shrubland along the Gascoyne River in Western Australia.

Threats. The survival of the Yinnietharra rock dragon is threatened by a number of problems, mostly involving *habitat* (living place). The vegetation that the rock dragon depends on for food and shelter has been disappearing as people in the Gascoyne River region have cleared the land for farming, pastureland, and housing developments. In addition, remaining undeveloped areas are now often separated by these developments. This problem, known as habitat fragmentation, makes it difficult for a *species*

Indian Ocean
Pacific Ocean
Coral Sea
Tropic of Capricorn
Great Australian Bight
Tasman Sea

Yinnietharra rock dragon

(types of animal) to thrive, because there are few or no ways for the animal to spread to new areas.

Another problem is the collection of rocks from the rock dragon's habitat. People collect and sell attractively shaped rocks, called "bush rocks," from the area for use in landscaping yard walls and gardens. They also collect the rocks for industrial and *commercial* (business) uses. As bush rocks disappear, the dragons lose their spots for basking and hiding.

The Yinnietharra rock dragon is actually a shy creature who runs for cover at the first sign of an intruder.

Large ground (Grand) skink

Oligosoma grande

Conservation status: Vulnerable (IUCN)
Nationally endangered (NZTCS)

The large ground skink—also known as the grand skink—is one of the largest lizards in New Zealand. This skink is also one of the rarest reptiles in either New Zealand or Australia. It is found only in an area called Otago on the South Island, one of the two main islands that make up New Zealand.

The large ground skink lives in areas with tall clumps of grass growing between outcrops of coarse rock. Large cracks in the rocks shelter the lizard from hot temperatures and predators.

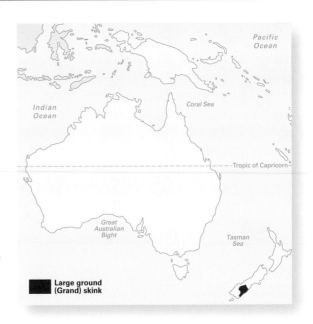

Large ground (Grand) skink

Appearance. The large ground skink may grow to a length of 11 inches (28 centimeters). Its short-legged body is mainly black with many yellowish flecks. This color combination serves as a type of *camouflage* (protection that makes the animal less visible). In this way, the reptile can hide among the dark lichen-covered rocks found throughout its *habitat* (living place).

Daily life. Large ground skinks are most often seen during the daytime, especially when it is sunny. They may scamper over rock surfaces or across the grassy ground in search of insects, fruits, or other food. These reptiles are *omnivores*—that is, they eat a wide variety of plants and animals.

Large ground skinks are able to breed when they reach the age of four. Females have from two to four young each year. But only about 60 percent of the young survive to adulthood.

Still, for a lizard, the large ground skink has a rather lengthy lifespan. Some have lived more than 17 years in the wild. In *captivity* (zoos or other places in which animals are kept for safety or dislay and sometimes bred), they may live even longer.

Threats. The large ground skink's remaining habitat is only a small remnant of its original *range* (area in which an animal naurally lives). Various human activities—including mining, forestry, and agriculture—have destroyed much of the lizard's original habitat. Unfortunately, large ground skinks seem to have little natural fear of predators and so are easy prey for cats, stoats, weasels, ferrets, and hedgehogs introduced to the region by people.

Conservation. Conservationists established a recovery plan in the 1990's to help protect populations of wild large ground skinks. The plan also was designed to help another threatened species in the same region called the Otago skink.

Part of the plan involves breeding the lizards in *captivity* (zoos and other protected places) to build up the size of the populations, with the goal of releasing many of the animals into protected reserves in the wild. Another part of the plan involves trapping mammals, particularly *feral* (formerly tamed) cats, that prey on large ground skinks.

The large ground skink makes for an easy meal because the lizard seems to have little natural fear of cats and other predators introduced to its habitat by people.

Paradisaea rudolphi

Conservation status: Vulnerable

One of the world's most beautiful birds, the blue bird-of-paradise has bright blue feathers on its wings, back, and tail. It has a black head, white rings around the eyes, and a white bill. The male has two long, thin, ribbonlike streamers extending from the tail. The bird grows to a length of about 12 inches (30 centimeters), including its tail.

Habitat. The blue bird-of-paradise lives in moist mountain forests in Papua New Guinea. It feeds on fruits high in the forest *canopy* (tree tops). The birds may leave their mountain forests to search for fruit in gardens, orchards, and other residential and agricultural areas in nearby valleys. People there often hear them singing.

Mating displays. The male birds are famous for their mating displays. Each male claims his own small area of ground, called a *lek,* in which to display to passing females. During this mating display, he struts around making a slow and rhythmic "wahr, wahr, wahr" call.

After a time, the male flies up into a tree, where he hangs upside down on a branch. He fully spreads his magnificent blue wings and belts out a metallic humming call. He may also make croaking and growling sounds. As his body sways back and forth, he rhythmically expands and contracts a black oval with a red border at the center of his chest. The display may last for hours.

Threats. Biologists are not sure how many blue birds-of-paradise exist in the wild, but estimates range from about 3,500 to 15,000. Whatever the exact number, biologists believe that the bird's numbers are gradually declining. One major reason is hunting of the birds for their colorful plumage, especially their chest and tail feathers. The male's long streamers are especially prized. The bird's feathers are used

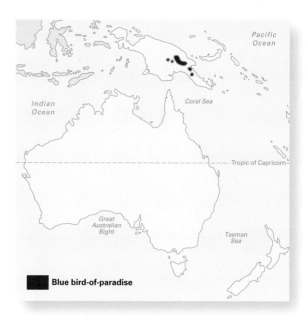

Blue bird-of-paradise

by local tribes for traditional practices. They are also sold to tourists—despite a ban on the practice.

Another reason for the bird's decline is the growth in the human population in the region. People are increasingly expanding residential and agricultural developments into the bird's natural *habitat* (living place). Fortunately, the blue bird-of-paradise is able to tolerate more habitat disturbances than many other threatened *species* (types) can withstand. For this reason, the IUCN classifies the species as *Vulnerable* rather than the more serious *Endangered*.

Conservation. The government of Papua New Guinea has passed a number of laws to protect the blue bird-of-paradise. However, government officials have a hard time enforcing these laws because most of the bird's habitat is owned by traditional tribes. Members of these tribes often hunt the bird for its spectacular feathers.

The male blue bird-of-paradise is known for his spectacular feathers and streamers and his elaborate mating display.

Pezoporus occidentalis

Conservation status: Endangered (IUCN & EPBC)

The night parrot looks like the typical bird that many people picture when they think of a parrot. Its body is bright green with a yellow belly and black-and-yellow streaks and spots. On the underside of each wing is a whitish-yellowish bar. The bird is about 9 inches (23 centimeters) long and has a wingspan of about 17.7 inches (45 centimeters).

Given up for extinction. *Ornithologists* (scientists who study birds) consider the night parrot one of the most mysterious and hard-to-find birds in the world. During the mid-1900's, they thought the bird was extinct, because no one had reported seeing one since 1912. Then there was a confirmed sighting in 1979. The bird has been seen since then, but its appearances are few and far between.

The first confirmed photographs of the night parrot were not reported until 2013, when a photographer showed several photos and a brief video that he took in the western part of the state of Queensland. He said that he spent thousands of hours over a period of 15 years looking for this parrot *species* (type) before he finally found it!

Habitat. Night parrots favor dry and semidry *habitats* (living places). They are believed to nest in clumps of such low-growing plants as hummock grass and chenopod shrubs. Besides Queensland, the night parrot has been spotted elsewhere in Australia, including in the Pilbara region of Western Australia.

Habits. As suggested by its name, the night parrot is *nocturnal*—that is, active in the cool conditions of nighttime. Limiting activity to the night helps the bird conserve water in its dry habitat. Some biologists believe that the parrot may get almost all the water it needs from the plant food that it eats, such as grass seeds.

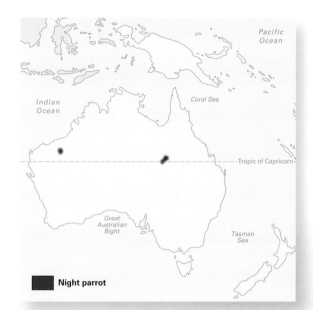

Night parrot

But other biologists believe that the bird frequently visits waterholes or other sources of water to drink.

Threats. Because the bird is sighted so rarely, little is known with certainty about the behaviors and habits of the night parrot. This lack of firm information also makes it difficult to correctly estimate its population size or trends. However, biologists speculate that the population of these ground-nesting parrots may be declining as a result of predation by foxes and such *feral* animals as cats brought to the region by people. (Feral animals are those from a tamed species that have reverted to their original or wild condition.) In addition, the grassy and shrubby habitat of the parrots has been damaged by livestock grazing and large wildfires.

Night parrots shelter in clumps of grass in a hand-colored lithograph from *The Birds of Australia* (1840-1848) by English scientist and artist John Gould. The seven-volume work—the first comprehensive survey of the continent's birds—included information on some 680 birds, more than 300 of which were previously unknown to scientists.

Chloebia gouldiae
Conservation status: Endangered

The Gouldian finch's alternate name—rainbow finch—does a much better job of describing the amazing colors of this little bird. Their heads may be black, red, or yellow-orange. They have green wings and back and a blue rump. Their chest is purple, and their belly is yellow. The finch's cone-shaped bill is whitish with a reddish tip, which makes it look as though the bird is wearing lipstick. The colors on males are bolder and brighter than those on females.

Mating dance. Male Gouldian finches perform a special courtship dance on tree limbs. The dance starts with the male bobbing his head, wiping his beak, and ruffling his feathers. He then holds his body and tail firm and straight, while he expands his chest and fluffs out his head feathers.

If the female is impressed enough with this display, she may respond with some beak-wiping of her own. After the pair mate and the female lays her eggs (usually from two to four), both parents care for the eggs and raise the young.

Habitat. Gouldian finches are seed-eating birds that live in open, grassy woodlands. The birds generally build their nests in tree hollows. Eucalyptus trees are a favorite nesting site.

Most of the finch's natural woodland *habitats* lie in northern Australia. (A habitat is the kind of environment in which an animal usually lives.)

Threats. Fewer than 2,500 adult Gouldian finches may live in the wild. The bird has become endangered mainly because of changes to its habitat. Grazing cattle and other livestock often eat or trample grasses that the finches depend on for seeds.

Wildfires and fires set by people have caused additional habitat problems by

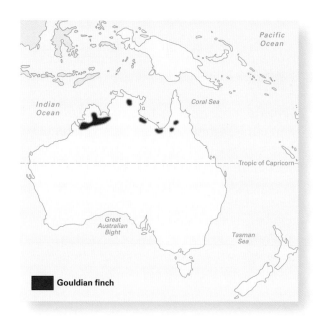

Gouldian finch

destroying grass before the plants can produce seed heads. The fires also make it difficult for the finches to nest, as they are less likely to nest in holes inside burnt trees.

Another big problem has been trapping of the uniquely colored Gouldian finches for sale as pets or as display birds in *aviaries* (large cages or buildings where wild birds are kept). However, trapping has been banned since the 1980's. Biologists believe that infections with a parasitic mite in the past also claimed many wild finches.

Conservation. Many biologists believe that the wild Gouldian finch population began to *stabilize* (stop declining in number) in the 2000's as a result of conservation efforts. Because the finch was collected so widely, many captive populations of the bird exist around the world.

The Gouldian finch dazzles with its brilliant and varied colors. Its tail feathers end in a sharp point.

Eudyptes schlegeli

Conservation status: Vulnerable

The royal penguin is a so-called crested penguin, with long yellow crests, or plumes, above the eyes. Its crests are similar to those of a related penguin called the macaroni penguin. Some people think that the crests on these birds look like macaroni noodles. The macaroni and royal penguins are sometimes classified as the same *species* (type).

The royal penguin has an orange bill and the typical black-and-white "tuxedo" coloration of most penguins. Standing approximately 2.3 feet (70 centimeters) tall, it is a medium-sized penguin. Females are usually a bit shorter than males.

Habitat. During their breeding season, the penguins live on Macquarie Island, as well as two nearby Pacific islands, about halfway between New Zealand and Antarctica. They nest in large colonies, laying their eggs on level rocky or sandy ground. During the rest of the year, they swim to other areas to search for food. They have been sighted in waters from Tasmania, off the southeastern coast of Australia, to Antarctica. Royal penguins eat fish, squid, and shrimplike *crustaceans* (hard-shelled animals) called euphausiids.

Commercial importance. During the 1800's and early 1900's, royal penguins and other penguin species were hunted for important manufactured products. Millions of the seabirds were killed for their fat, which was used for fuel in lamps to provide light and for tanning leather. The penguins were also killed to get their feathers, which were used for clothing decorations, and for their skins, which were used to make caps, slippers, purses, and other products.

The mass killing of the penguins stopped only after cheaper and better alternatives to animal fat became available. These alternatives included petroleum products and *synthetic* (artificially made) fabrics.

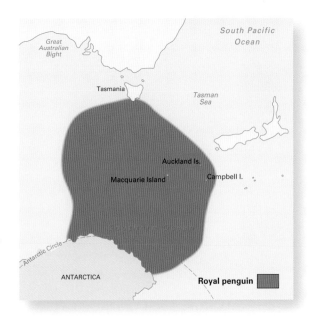

Stable but fragile. The royal penguin population has recovered and is currently believed to be stable, with more than 1 million individuals. However, the IUCN still classifies the species as *Vulnerable,* mainly because of the penguin's extremely limited breeding *range.* (A range is the area in which an animal naturally lives.) Such a small range for reproduction leaves the penguin extremely vulnerable to a natural or environmental disaster, such as a serious oil spill, that could wipe them out.

Threats. Royal penguins face a number of continuing threats. Among these are rats that eat their eggs and young; plastic debris that kills the penguins that eat it; and even researchers and tourists who disturb the birds. In addition, *commercial* (business) fishing operations in the Antarctic have greatly reduced the numbers of the fish the penguins prey on.

During the breeding season, royal penguins form large colonies of up to 500,000 pairs, mainly on Macquarie Island. Scientists are not sure where the migratory birds live during the rest of the year.

Pteropus anetianus

Conservation status: Vulnerable

Flying foxes are actually bats with foxlike faces. These large brownish, blackish, or grayish mammals live in forests and swamps on the Vanuatu *archipelago*, near New Guinea, in the South Pacific Ocean. (An archipelago is a broad expanse of sea with a large number of islands.)

Appearance. Vanuatu flying foxes have large eyes and long, oval ears. The bats have a wingspan that is about 30 inches (76 centimeters) wide. They *roost* (rest or sleep) in small colonies in trees.

Diet. Like most other flying foxes, Vanuatu flying foxes eat mainly fruits, including figs, coconuts, and breadfruit, a tropical fruit with a starchy pulp that tastes somewhat like bread.

The bats find the fruit using their sharp senses of sight and smell. Their powerful jaws and large canine teeth—their fangs—help them break into the tough rinds of fruit. They may bite into the fruit while hovering in the air or holding onto a branch with one foot and pressing the fruit against their chest with the other foot. They sometimes hang upside down while eating.

The bats often squeeze fruit with their mouth to drink the fruit juices. They may then spit out the fruit's pulp and seeds. The animals have long tongues to help them reach deep inside flowers to get at nectar. They may also eat insects to supplement their diet.

Threats. The frequent visits of these bats to flowers mean that flying foxes help pollinate flowers and *disperse* (spread) seeds for various kinds of plants. But they sometimes visit farms, where they can cause a lot of damage to fruit crops. For this reason, Vanuatu flying foxes are sometimes killed as agricultural pests. But local people more commonly hunt and kill the large bats for food.

Vanuatu flying fox

Another threat to the *species* (type) is the loss of their forest *habitat* (living place). These areas have been greatly reduced in size as they have been replaced by agricultural and residential developments. This habitat destruction has wiped out many of the bats' foraging and roosting sites.

Natural disasters, including typhoons, volcanic eruptions, and earthquakes, occur frequently in the Vanuatu archipelago. These disasters, along with habitat disturbances caused by people, pose the main threats to the survival of the Vanuatu flying fox. Some scientists are concerned that rising sea levels and flooding linked to climate change will make these problems worse.

In addition, Vanuatu flying foxes do not often disperse to new areas. So when one part of their habitat is threatened or destroyed, the bats there are likely to die out. Despite the many challenges faced by Vanuatu flying foxes, biologists believe that their population is not yet seriously endangered.

Vanuatu flying foxes are actually bats. They roost in small groups in trees.

Aproteles bulmerae

Conservation status: Critically Endangered

Scientists learned about these bats from fossils before they ever saw the bats in the wild. In fact, scientists thought the bat had become extinct some 12,000 years ago. Then in 1975, thousands of the bats were discovered *roosting* (sleeping or resting) inside a remote mountain cave surrounded by forest in the far western part of Papua New Guinea. Soon afterward, local people killed most of the bats with shotguns to get their meat.

Unfortunately, only a small number of Bulmer's fruit bats have been found at other sites in the region. Scientists consider Bulmer's fruit bat to be one of the rarest and most endangered bat *species* (type) in the world. There may be fewer than 250 adults in the wild.

Acrobatic bat. The Bulmer's fruit bat is unusual in several ways. It is the largest bat species known to roost inside caves. It is also one of the few bats that can hover and fly backward.

Appearance. The body of a Bulmer's fruit bat may grow up to 9 1/2 inches (24 centimeters) long and weigh roughly 1.3 pounds (600 grams). The bat has an average wingspan of about 3.3 feet (1 meter).

Hunting. Bulmer's fruit bats leave their cave at dusk to forage for fruit. They are very cautious animals. If the first few bats that fly out happen to notice any people or other possible threats in the area, they will return to the cave. They will then wait to leave until the coast is clear.

The bats sometimes fly great distances to find food before returning to the cave before sunrise. Scientists observed one female feeding 20 miles (32 kilometers) from her roost. Females carry their young with them on foraging trips until the young are old enough to fly—typically about four or five weeks after birth.

Bulmer's fruit bat

Threats. The main threat to the survival of the Bulmer's fruit bat is hunters who kill them for their meat. In addition, the bats—like other bat species—are highly sensitive to any kind of disturbance to their roosts. The most sensitive time is when mother bats are *nursing* (feeding milk to) their young. If people enter roosting caves at that time, the mothers may become so upset that they abandon their young, leaving them to die. Yet another threat to the bat population is wildfires, which can seriously damage the bats' forest *habitat* (living place).

Conservation. Conservationists believe that the Bulmer's fruit bat would benefit from a captive-breeding program. Such a program would at least ensure the survival of the species if it should disappear from the wild. Some conservationists have also suggested moving some of the bats to another, perhaps safer, part of the New Guinea forest.

The Bulmer's fruit bat, one of the world's rarest and most endangered bats, is also the largest bat known to roost inside caves.

Tasmanian devil

Sarcophilus harrisii
Conservation status: Endangered

The Tasmanian devil is the largest meat-eating *marsupial*. (A marsupial is a mammal that carries its incompletely developed young inside a pouch in which the young are *nursed* [fed milk].) Adult Tasmanian devils are about 3 feet (0.9 meter) long, with mostly black fur and some white markings. They have short, muscular legs and a large head.

Named for screeches. Early European settlers on Tasmania—the Australian island-state on which the devil lives—gave this animal its scary name because of the loud screeches and snarls it makes during the night. These noises are usually made when two or more devils are competing or fighting for the same food. In most cases, the devil with the nastiest-sounding display wins, and the competitor leaves peacefully. Tasmanian devils are actually shy and cautious animals that seek to avoid fights.

Tasmanian devils typically get their food by scavenging for *carcasses* (dead bodies of animals). They find this food with their sensitive sense of smell. Their powerful jaws enable them to break through even the largest bones. During their nighttime searches for carcasses, they also sometimes hunt and kill small mammals, birds, reptiles, and insects.

Young devils. A female devil gives birth to two to four tiny, naked young, which then crawl into the mother's abdominal pouch to nurse. They stay in the pouch for about 15 weeks, getting larger and growing fur. They then crawl out of the pouch and start living in a grass-lined den. They move away to live on their own when they are about 10 months old.

Threats. Tasmanian devils used to live on additional islands in the region. However, they were eliminated from those islands, and their numbers were greatly reduced on Tasmania.

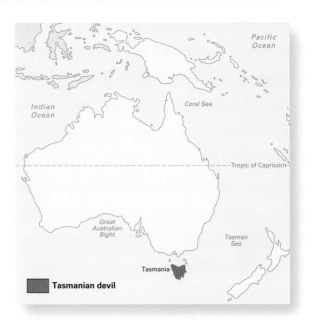

Tasmanian devil

The main cause of the population plummet was farmers who trapped and poisoned the devils to keep them away from livestock. The Australian government banned the killing of Tasmanian devils in the 1940's. But people also destroyed much of the devil's forest *habitat* (living place). Other reasons for the drop in the number of Tasmanian devils include killings by automobiles and by domestic dogs. These dangers claim hundreds of devils every year.

Cancer epidemic. Since the 1990's, an infectious kind of cancer called devil facial tumor disease has killed tens of thousands of the animals. The disease is spread by biting, scratching, and sexual contact.

In response, Australian and Tasmanian officials established the Save the Tasmanian Devil Program. Scientists with the program are isolating groups of devils to keep them from developing the disease. They are also working to develop a test to identify devils with the virus before they become infectious.

The Tasmanian devil was named for the frightening screams and snarls it makes while mating or competing for food.

Lagostrophus fasciatus

Conservation status: Endangered (IUCN)
Vulnerable (EPBC)

The banded hare wallaby is a small *marsupial*. It is a little less than 1.5 feet (0.5 meters) long, not counting a tail of about the same length. (A marsupial is a mammal that carries its incompletely developed young inside a pouch in which the young are *nursed* [fed milk].) The banded hare wallaby is the last surviving member of a group of animals called short-faced kangaroos that went extinct about 40,000 years ago. One member of this group was the largest kangaroo that ever lived. It stood about 9.8 feet (3 meters) tall.

Appearance. The banded hare wallaby has thick, shaggy gray fur with dark stripes (or bands) on its lower back. Those stripes led some people to think, incorrectly, that the animal was a type of raccoon.

Daily life. Banded hare wallabies huddle together in groups beneath low trees or shrubs during the day. They come out to feed on grasses and shrubs at night.

Habitat. The banded hare wallaby once lived throughout southwestern Australia but became extinct there in the early 1900's. It disappeared from the mainland because settlers cleared much of its natural shrubby-grassy *habitat* (living area) for farmland. The wallaby was also forced to compete for plant food with sheep and rabbits introduced by people. In addition, cats and other nonnative predators killed many of the animals.

Today, wild banded hare wallabies can be found only on the islands of Dorre and Bernier in Shark Bay, about 30 miles (50 kilometers) off the coast of Western Australia. Scientists have introduced a small population of the animals onto nearby Faure Island.

Threats. The survival of the banded hare wallaby in its remaining island homes is threatened

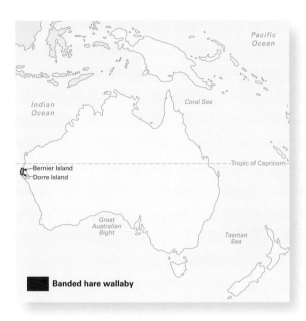

Banded hare wallaby

by a number of factors. These factors include predation by introduced cats and foxes, habitat destruction by fire, and the spread of disease.

The banded hare wallaby's population naturally *fluctuates* (increases and decreases) because of changes in weather. The population tends to increase following rainy periods and decrease following dry periods. Severe *droughts* (dry spells) have caused especially great harm to the *species* (type) by killing the hare wallaby's plant food and cover. These natural fluctuations may be worsened by warming temperatures and other ongoing climate changes that nearly all scientists believe are caused mainly by the burning of *fossil fuels* (coal, oil, natural gas).

Conservation. Conservationists have tried to introduce captive-bred banded hare wallabies to mainland Australia and other islands besides Faure. However, the animals in those reintroduction attempts died from a combination of predators, drought, and other challenges.

Banded hare wallaby populations are strongly influenced by the weather. After dry periods, their numbers fall, as grasses and other food disappear.

Bettongia penicillata

Conservation status: Critically Endangered

The Aboriginal People of Australia have told stories about the woylie, also known as the brush-tailed rat-kangaroo, for hundreds of years. The stories reveal that this small rodentlike *marsupial* used to live throughout much of Australia, in such *habitats* (living places) as deserts, grasslands, and forests. (A marsupial is a mammal that carries its incompletely developed young inside a pouch in which the young are *nursed* [fed milk].) Today, however, this *species* (type) is found mainly in the forests and woodlands of southwestern Australia.

Appearance. The woylie has a grayish-brown body that is about 15 inches (38 centimeters) long and a tail that is a little shorter. The animal eats mostly plant food, such as seeds and roots, but it has also been seen feeding on dead animals. It hides and rests in nests of sticks and leaves, which it builds under shrubs or next to tree trunks.

Threats and decline. Populations of woylies began to decline as the European *colonization* (settlement) of Australia expanded in the 1800's. The European colonists converted natural environment into agricultural land and other developments, and they killed the woylies as pests.

Recent severe population declines are related to a number of old and new problems. These problems include continued habitat destruction, competition for plant food with grazing livestock, and the spread of diseases. Many woylies have been killed by red foxes and cats introduced to Australia by European settlers. Scientists believe that more research is needed to better understand the causes of the species's recent population declines.

Conservation. The remaining *range* of the woylie in Australia includes some nature

Woylie

reserves. (A range is the area in which an animal naturally lives.) Woylies have become extinct in the states of South Australia and New South Wales.

Since the 1970's, conservationists have tried to reintroduce the species to these states and onto some Australian islands. In some cases, the animals have survived and reproduced. In other cases, the animals died. Still other efforts are ongoing, and so scientists don't know whether they are working. Despite the species's protection in nature reserves and the limited success of reintroduction programs, the woylie remains a critically endangered species.

Since the 1990's in Western Australia, conservationists have also tried to protect the woylie by controlling the population of the nonnative red foxes. These efforts have led to big increases in the numbers and distribution of woylies in this region. Biologists believe that continued fox control is important to ensure the woylie's survival. They argue that the cat population also needs to be better controlled.

The woylie stands and hops on its sturdy hind legs. Its small forearms are usually held close to its pale white belly.

Lasiorhinus krefftii

Conservation status: Critically Endangered (IUCN) Endangered (EPBC)

With a stocky body more than 39 inches (100 centimeters) long, the northern hairy-nosed wombat is one of the world's largest burrowing mammals. This grayish or brownish *marsupial* has strong front legs and large clawed forepaws that allow it to dig the long, deep burrows in which it lives. (A marsupial is a mammal that carries its incompletely developed young inside a pouch in which the young are *nursed* [fed milk].)

The northern hairy-nosed wombat gets its name from the long, white whiskers that extend from the side of its nose. These sensitive whiskers help the wombat find its way around in its dark, underground living spaces.

Burrows. The wombats make their burrows in deep, sandy soil, usually along rivers in woodlands or grasslands. They spend most of the day there. Although the wombats typically live alone and keep to themselves, several individuals may share a large, complex burrow system. Each wombat marks its main part of the burrow system with urine and dung. The animals come out of their burrows at night to forage on grasses. In winter, they sometimes come to the surface to warm themselves by basking in the sun.

Habitat. The northern hairy-nosed wombat is the rarest of the three *species* (types) of wombat—and one of the rarest mammals of any kind in the world. It used to live throughout much of eastern Australia. However, many wild populations of the animals vanished during the 1900's. The species survives today only in a small part of Epping Forest National Park, in central Queensland.

Threats. The main causes of the drop in the wombat's numbers have been competition for grasses with grazing cattle, sheep, and rabbits; killings by dingoes and other predators; worsening *droughts* (severe dry spells); and a loss of natural *habitat* (living place) to agriculture and other human developments.

Conservation. Conservation efforts to protect the northern hairy-nosed wombat began in the early 1970's, when Epping Forest National Park was set up as a natural refuge. Other conservation actions have included the banning of livestock from wombat habitat and the building of fences to protect wombats from dingo predators. Conservationists also have plans to breed wombats in *captivity* (zoos and other places in which animals are kept for safety or display and sometimes bred). These captive-bred wombats would then be released into the wild. However, much more scientific research and conservation actions are needed to ensure the survival of this critically endangered species.

Hairy-nosed wombats were once widespread. But their populations have decreased greatly due to loss of habitat and competition for food with livestock and rabbits.

Myrmecobius fasciatus

Conservation status: Endangered (IUCN)
Vulnerable (EPBC)

The numbat is a small, graceful *marsupial* with a unique appearance. (A marsupial is a mammal that carries its incompletely developed young inside a pouch in which the young are *nursed* [fed milk].) It has a slender reddish-brown body, about 10 inches (25 centimeters) long, with black and white stripes across its back and rump. A bold, black stripe marks the side of the head from snout to ear. The animal's tail is long and bushy.

Female numbats are unusual among marsupials in not having an enclosed pouch for their young. Instead, the mothers carry their young in an open pouch that has long guard hairs to warm and protect their babies. The young cling to the mother's hair and nipples.

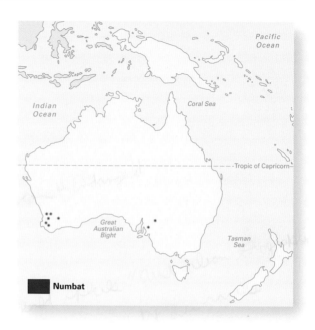

Numbat

Behavior. The numbat also displays unusual behaviors. Unlike most marsupials, which are *nocturnal* (active at night), numbats are active during the daytime. They walk around with their narrow snout to the ground, smelling for the shallow underground tunnels of termites. When they detect the hidden insects, they use their front claws to scratch open the tunnels. They then use their long, sticky tongue to lick up the insects. According to some estimates, a numbat may eat as many as 20,000 termites every day. They sometimes also eat ants.

During the night, numbats usually rest inside hollow logs, underground burrows made by other animals, or other sheltered places, hidden from predators. Two of their most dangerous enemies are introduced, or nonnative, red foxes and domestic cats. If a numbat's shelter is discovered by a predator, the numbat may use its rear end to block the entrance. The skin on its rear end is thick, so even if a predator bites it, the numbat will probably survive.

Habitat. Numbats live mainly in *semiarid* (somewhat dry) scrubby woodlands dominated by eucalyptus shrubs and trees. Before the 1900's, numbats were common throughout southern Australia. But today they are found only in the southwestern corner and south central area of the country.

Threats. Numbat populations have fallen greatly as their natural woodland *habitat* (living place) has been cleared for agricultural developments. Predators—not only red foxes and cats, but also dogs and dingoes—have further reduced numbat numbers. Frequent large fires in some areas have burned up the dead logs that numbats prefer for shelter.

Conservation. The numbat is the official emblem of the state of Western Australia. Various laws passed to preserve this endangered *species* (type) have led to a reduction in the fox population and the establishment of nature reserves. Scientists have also reintroduced numbats to areas from which they had disappeared.

The number of numbats has fallen dramatically because of habitat change and attacks from introduced animals.

Glossary

Archipelago A broad expanse of sea with a large number of islands.

Aviary A building or large cage for many birds, especially wild birds.

Brackish Slightly salty.

Bycatch Animals accidentally swept up by fishers trying to catch more desirable food fish.

Camouflage Coloration or other physical traits that protect an animal by making the animal hard to see.

Canopy The top layer of the trees in a forest.

Captivity Refers to a zoo or other nonnatural place in which animals are kept for safety or display and sometimes bred.

Carcass The dead body of an animal.

Caterpillar A wormlike creature that is the second stage in the life history of butterflies and moths.

Colonization The settlement of a continent or other region by certain people.

Commercial Having to do with businesses and making money.

Crustacean An invertebrate animal with many jointed legs and a hard external shell.

Degrade Reduce in quality.

Disperse Spread.

Drought A long period of dry weather.

Ecosystem A community of plants and animals and their *abiotic* (nonliving or physical) environment, including climate, soil, water, air, nutrients, and energy.

Feral Refers to animals from a tamed species that have reverted to their original or wild condition.

Fluctuate To increase and decrease.

Habitat The type of environment in which an organism usually lives.

Hermaphrodite An animal or a plant that has both male and female reproductive organs.

Incubate To protect eggs, usually by sitting on them, and keep them warm so that they will hatch.

Invertebrate An animal without a backbone.

Lek A meeting ground in which male birds gather, display their plumage, and court females.

Marsupial A mammal that carries its incompletely developed young inside a pouch in which the young are nursed.

Metamorphosis The process in which certain animals change in physical form from an immature stage to a mature stage, such as a tadpole changing into a frog.

Molt To shed a hard, outer covering called the exoskeleton.

Nocturnal Active at night.

Nurse To drink milk from a mother animal's *teats* (nipples).

Omnivore An animal that eats a wide variety of both animal and vegetable food.

Organic Refers to matter that was produced from plants or animals.

Ornithologist A scientist who specializes in the study of birds.

Outback The rural interior of Australia and its unique characteristics.

Placenta An organ in a pregnant mammal's womb that provides nourishment to the unborn young.

Range An area in which an animal or plant occurs naturally.

Roosting The resting or sleeping of birds.

Sediment Soil, stones, and other matter that flows into a body of water and becomes suspended in the water or settles to the bottom.

Semiarid Lands that are somewhat dry, but not as dry as a desert.

Species A group of animals or plants that have certain permanent characteristics in common and are able to interbreed.

Stabilize Stop declining in number.

Synthetic Artificially made.

Tadpole An immature frog or toad; also called a polliwog.

Toxic Poisonous.

Books

Animal Encyclopedia: 2,500 Animals with Photos, Maps, and More! Washington, D.C.: National Geographic, 2012. Print.

Hammond, Paula. *The Atlas of Endangered Animals: Wildlife Under Threat Around the World.* Tarrytown, NY: Marshall Cavendish, 2010. Print.

Hoare, Ben, and Tom Jackson. *Endangered Animals.* New York: DK Pub., 2010. Print.

Silhol, Sandrine, Gaëlle Guérive, and Marie Doucedame. *Extraordinary Endangered Animals.* New York: Abrams Books for Young Readers, 2011. Print.

Weston, Christopher, and Art Wolfe. *Animals on the Edge: Reporting from the Frontline of Extinction.* New York: Thames & Hudson, 2009. Print.

Websites

Arkive. Wildscreen, 2014. Web. 14 May 2014.

"Australian Wildlife." *BBC Nature.* BBC, 2014. Web. 21 May 2014.

Foundation for Australia's Most Endangered Species (FAME). FAME, 2012. Web. 21 May 2014.

Jantos, Julian. "Australia's most endangered species." *Australian Geographic.* Ninemsn, 2 Oct. 2012. Web. 21 May 2014.

"N.Z. Birds and Animals." *Christchurch City Libraries.* Christchurch City Libraries, n.d. Web. 21 May 2014.

TerraNature. TerraNature Trust, 2013. Web. 21 May 2014.

Tregaskis, Shiona. "The world's extinct and endangered species – interactive map." *The Guardian.* Guardian News and Media Limited, 3 Sept. 2012. Web. 14 May 2014.

Organizations *for helping endangered animals*

Foundation for Australia's Most Endangered Species (FAME)
FAME is an organization dedicated to helping Australian species most at risk of extinction.
http://fame.org.au/

Defenders of Wildlife
Founded in 1947, Defenders of Wildlife is a major national conservation organization focused on wildlife and habitat conservation.
http://www.defenders.org/take-action

National Geographic – Big Cats Initiative
National Geographic, along with Dereck and Beverly Joubert, launched the Big Cats Initiative to raise awareness and implement change to the dire situation facing big cats.
http://animals.nationalgeographic.com/animals/big-cats-initiative/

National Geographic – The Ocean Initiative
National Geographic's Ocean Initiative helps identify and support individuals and organizations that are using creative and entrepreneurial approaches to marine conservation.
http://ocean.nationalgeographic.com/ocean/about-ocean-initiative

National Wildlife Federation – Adoption Center
Symbolically adopt your favorite species and at the same time support the National Wildlife Federation's important work protecting wildlife and connecting people to nature.
http://www.shopnwf.org/Adoption-Center/index.cat

Neighbor Ape
Neighbor Ape strives to conserve the habitat of wild chimpanzees in southeastern Senegal, to protect the chimpanzees themselves, and to provide for the wellbeing of the Senegalese people who have traditionally lived in the area alongside these chimpanzees.
http://www.globalgiving.org/donate/10235/neighbor-ape/

Smithsonian National Zoo – Adopt a Species
The Adopt a Species program supports the National Zoo's extraordinary work in the conservation and care of the world's rarest animals.
http://nationalzoo.si.edu/support/adoptspecies/

World Wildlife Fund
World Wildlife Fund works in 100 countries and is supported by over 1 million members in the United States and close to 5 million globally.
http://www.worldwildlife.org/how-to-help

Index

Acknowledgments

The publishers acknowledge the following sources for illustrations. Credits read from top to bottom, left to right, on their respective pages. All maps, charts, and diagrams were prepared by the staff unless otherwise noted.

COVER © Melinda Moore, Getty Images; © Karl Johaentges, Alamy Images
4 © Karl Johaentges, Alamy Images
7 © Biosphoto/SuperStock
9 © Oxford Scientific/Getty Images
11 © Dr. Beverley Van Praagh
12 © Dr. Richard Pillans
13 © Jeff Whitty
15 © Marine Themes
17 © Aaron Payne
19 © Minden Pictures/SuperStock
21 © Steve Wilson
23 © Neil Fitzgerald
25 © Tim Laman, National Geographic/ SuperStock
27 © Alamy Images
29 © James Urbach, Purestock/Alamy Images
31 © Animals Animals/SuperStock
33 © Michele Westmorland, Nature Picture Library; © B.G. Thomson, Science Source
35 © Peter Schouten
37 © Juniors/SuperStock
38 © Tony Brown
41 © Minden Pictures/SuperStock
43 © Dave Watts, Nature Picture Library
45 © Ann & Steve Toon, Alamy Images

DATE DUE